NEIL DeGRASSE TYSON

JENNIFER CULP

ROSEN
PUBLISHING®

New York

Published in 2015 by The Rosen Publishing Group, Inc.
29 East 21st Street, New York, NY 10010

First Edition

Library of Congress Cataloging-in-Publication Data

Culp, Jennifer.
Neil deGrasse Tyson/Jennifer Culp.
      pages cm. — (Great science writers)
Includes bibliographical references and index.
ISBN 978-1-4777-7691-9 (library bound)
1. Tyson, Neil deGrasse—Juvenile literature. 2. Astrophysicists
—United States—Biography—Juvenile literature.
3. Astronautics—United States—Juvenile literature.
4. Universe—Juvenile literature. I. Title.
QB460.72.T97C85 2014
523.01092—dc23
[B]
                                                      2013043307

Manufactured in China

CONTENTS

INTRODUCTION

Neil deGrasse Tyson is an astrophysicist who researches star formation, exploding stars, dwarf galaxies, and the structure of our Milky Way, among other things. He is director of the Hayden Planetarium in New York City, he has served on two presidentially appointed commissions to advise the United States about space exploration, and he has been honored with the NASA Distinguished Public Service Medal, the highest award given by NASA to a nongovernment citizen.

In addition to his professional publications on his research, Tyson is well known for writing about science for the general public. His writings have reached millions of people who otherwise might never have been interested in the cosmos if not for Tyson's enthusiasm, wit, and ability to explain difficult concepts in a simple, understandable fashion. For a decade, Tyson wrote monthly essays for *Natural History* magazine and a monthly question-and-answer column for *StarDate* magazine. He has written ten books, including *Origins: Fourteen Billion Years of Cosmic Evolution* (cowritten with Donald Goldsmith), *Death by Black Hole: And Other Cosmic Quandaries,*

Neil deGrasse Tyson, seen here holding the world in his hands, has dedicated his life to learning about the universe and teaching others about its wonders.

The Pluto Files: The Rise and Fall of America's Favorite Planet, Space Chronicles: Facing the Ultimate Frontier, and his memoir, *The Sky Is Not the Limit: Adventures of an Urban Astrophysicist*.

Fascinated by the mysteries of the night sky, Tyson dreamed of becoming an astrophysicist since he was a child. He devoted his life to learning about the universe and sharing that knowledge with others. In a society that depends upon scientific achievement but doesn't, many feel, do enough to encourage thorough scientific education, Tyson is passionate about working to improve science literacy among the general public. He is active on Twitter, where he shares science facts and jokes, and hosts the radio show *StarTalk* alongside celebrity guests. Television programs based on his books have appeared on public television, and he hosts the TV programs *NOVA ScienceNOW* and *Cosmos: A Spacetime Odyssey*.

Tyson's curiosity about the universe and his dedication to sharing his knowledge with others have shaped the course of his life, and his work has made the world a better-informed place. Hard work in the face of adversity marked Tyson's path to realizing his goals and dreams. This "path of most resistance" only made him more determined to succeed. Now, his greatest pleasure lies in assisting others in their own journeys of discovery.

In the following chapters, you'll learn about Tyson's early interest in science, the valuable lessons he learned throughout his education, and a few of the many, many fascinating cosmic topics he has written about over the course of his career. When it comes to astrophysics, the sky is *not* the limit. Tyson's cosmic curiosity is as great and all-consuming as the universe itself, and through his writings, he hopes to inspire the same sense of wonder in you.

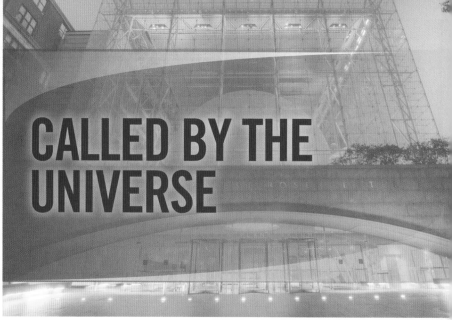

CHAPTER ONE

CALLED BY THE UNIVERSE

A visit to the Hayden Planetarium sky theater in Manhattan at the age of nine shaped the course of Neil deGrasse Tyson's entire life. "That was the night. I had been called," he wrote in his 2004 memoir, *The Sky Is Not the Limit: Adventures of an Urban Astrophysicist.* "The study of the universe would be my career, and no force on Earth would stop me. I was just nine years old, but I now had an answer for that perennially annoying question adults ask children, 'What do you want to be when you grow up?' Although I could barely pronounce the word, I would thenceforth reply, 'I want to be an astrophysicist.'"

Tyson did indeed grow up to become an astrophysicist, one of the best-known astrophysicists in the world, and is now the Frederick P. Rose Director of the Hayden Planetarium at the Rose Center for Earth

Tyson's long-held interests serve as a billboard for his knowledge about the universe. His extensive collection of cosmic ties has inspired compliments, criticism, and

and Space, the very place where he first discovered his own overwhelming interest in the universe. His path to becoming and then working as an astrophysicist was driven by hard work, luck, and an insatiable curiosity to learn ever more about the cosmos. Tyson had viewed the night sky from the rooftop of the Skyview Apartments in the Bronx where he lived as a child and worried that it wasn't truly as spectacular as the Hayden Planetarium's sky show indicated until a friend encouraged him to look at the moon through a pair of binoculars. Through their lenses, "the Moon was not just bigger, it was better," Tyson wrote. "The coal-dark shadows sharply revealed the Moon's surface to be three dimensional—a rich moonscape of mountains and valleys and craters and hills and plains. The Moon was no longer just a thing in the sky—it was another world. And if simple binoculars could transform the Moon, imagine what mountaintop telescopes could do with the rest of the universe."

A TELESCOPIC VIEW

Tyson's first telescope was a birthday gift from his parents, who encouraged his interest in the cosmos. The small 2.4-inch (61 millimeters) refractor with three eyepieces and a solar projection screen allowed twelve-year-old Tyson to observe the migration of sunspots across the sun's surface during the daytime and the stars and planets at night, just like Galileo Galilei, the first person to observe the planets through a telescope. Galileo built a telescope of his own design after hearing of its invention and immediately aimed it upward to observe the "wanderers": Mercury, Venus, Mars, Saturn, and Jupiter. (As Tyson explained in *Death by Black Hole: And Other Cosmic Quandaries*, it took humanity a while to realize that Earth, too, is one of the planets. Galileo's observations of the solar system in the early seventeenth century promoted acceptance of Nicolaus Copernicus's sun-centered model of the universe, which had caused great controversy more than a half-century earlier.) Before the invention of the telescope, the planets appeared as points of light in the sky just like the stars. Through his telescope, however, Galileo saw that they were actually spheres with distinctive features. He observed the phases of Venus and the moons of Jupiter, structures on the surface of the moon, and spots on the face of the sun. "When I, too, first saw these images I communed with Galileo across time and space," Tyson wrote in his memoir. "My cosmic discoveries, though old news for society, were as fresh for me in the Bronx, New York, as they must have been for Galileo in Florence, Italy, four centuries ago."

Albert Einstein wrote that Galileo Galilei *(pictured above)*, who lived from 1564 to 1642, is "the father of modern physics–indeed, of modern science

TYSON'S FAVORITE PLANET

The first heavenly body Tyson viewed through his first telescope was his favorite planet: Saturn. His particular fondness for the ringed planet is well-documented: "Of all the planets in the sky, my favorite is Saturn. Without question, debate or argument, Saturn is the most beautiful," he stated. In a middle school wood-shop class, Tyson labored to create a desk lamp in the shape of his favorite planet, which still resides on his desk today. At age fourteen, Tyson's fascination with Saturn allowed him to win a trivia contest over a ship-full of adult scientists. Here's what happened: In a class Tyson took after school at the Hayden Planetarium, he made the acquaintance of the director of education of the Explorer's Club of New York, who admired his youthful enthusiasm for the cosmos. Through this connection, Tyson was able to go on an Explorer's Club voyage to observe the total solar eclipse of 1973 off the coast of northwest Africa. Not your typical summer vacation for most teenagers! In his memoir, Tyson admitted he wouldn't have had the sense to make contact with the Explorer's Club director if his mother hadn't prompted him, and he lied and told others on the voyage that he was sixteen, rather than fourteen, to seem older and more experienced than he really was. In spite of his youth and relative lack of knowledge among the two thousand scientists, engineers, and eclipse enthusiasts onboard, Tyson's fondness for Saturn allowed his team to triumph in an astronomy trivia contest on the journey back home. Near the end of the contest, only two teams remained in the

running, including Tyson's. The final question was, "What feature of Saturn, other than its beautiful ring system, strongly distinguishes it from all other planets in the solar system?" As Tyson recounted: "I knew that my Saturn lamp, from seventh-grade

Saturn's rings (the feature that makes the planet Tyson's favorite) are composed of particles made of water ice and a small trace amount of rocky material. The rings of Saturn reflect light, increasing the planet's brightness.

wood shop, would float if you tossed it into a bathtub because it's made of wood. Wood is less dense than water. Saturn too would float if you could find a bathtub big enough to place it. Saturn is the only planet whose average density falls less than that of water." He delivered the winning answer, earning the applause of the room and a bottle of champagne for the adults at his table to enjoy. "Having gazed so long at the stars," he recalled, "I now had my first taste of being one—if only for a brief but effervescent moment." He later remarked on Saturn's unique density in *Death by Black Hole*: "In other words, a scoop of Saturn would float in your bathtub. Knowing this, I have always wanted for my bathtub entertainment a rubber Saturn instead of a rubber ducky."

PHYSICAL LAWS AS INTELLECTUAL ANCHORS

Ever excited to observe more features of the cosmos in greater detail, Tyson soon outgrew his first telescope. He worked as a dog walker to save up money to buy a larger 6-inch (152 mm) telescope, which he wrote, "looked like a cross between an artillery cannon and a grenade launcher." Unfortunately, nosy neighbors often imagined that the young black man they saw climbing to the roof to observe the sky was an armed burglar carrying a weapon. The police often arrived at his "observatory" in response to a neighbor's call. The majesty of the night sky often served Tyson on these occasions when he showed the police officers spectacular views through his telescope. "Saturn alone bailed me out a half dozen times," he wrote. This wouldn't be the last time Tyson was forced to deal with the consequences of racism on his journey to becoming an astrophysicist. In the face of unfairness and inconsistencies in society, however, the laws of physics remained knowable and constant. "The laws of physics apply everywhere on Earth and in the heavens, transcending social mores," Tyson stated in his memoir. "These same laws began to serve as one of my intellectual anchors amidst the irrationalities of society." In a 2000 essay for *Natural History* magazine entitled "On Earth as in the Heavens," he discussed this universality of physical laws. Isaac Newton's universal law of gravitation, which showed that the same force that causes apples to fall from trees also guides the orbits of all celestial bodies, drove a wave of scientific discovery. When laboratory prisms first allowed the light of the sun to be split into spectra, they revealed that the sun is made of the same chemical elements as those found on Earth—hydrogen, carbon, oxygen, nitrogen, and so forth. Jupiter's Great Red Spot, a "raging anti-cyclone that has been going strong for at least

350 years," owes its existence to the same physical processes that cause storms on Earth...and elsewhere in the solar system! Though solving the mystery of dark matter may eventually require adjustment to Newton's law of gravity, that's just the scientific process at work, not a change in the way the physics of the cosmos actually function. The universe continues to work independently of human understanding, while astrophysicists and other scientists attempt to discover as much as possible about it. Tyson summed up the concept simply in "On Earth as in the Heavens":

To the scientist, the universality of physical laws makes the cosmos a marvelously simple place. By comparison human nature—the psychologist's domain—is infinitely more daunting. In America, school boards vote on the subjects to be taught in the classroom, and in some cases these votes are cast according to the whims of social and political tides. Around the world, varying belief systems lead to political differences that are not always resolved

Tyson has little patience with those who would cling to irrational beliefs in the face of scientific evidence and even less tolerance for people who seek to profit off of others' ignorance and gullibility.

AMERICAN

peacefully. And some people talk to bus stop stanchions. The miracle of physical laws is that they apply everywhere, whether or not you choose to believe in them. Furthermore, that it's not a function of your mental health. After the laws of physics, everything else is opinion.

HARD WORK AND SUPPORT

Unfairnesses other than systemic racism could have adversely affected Tyson's ambition to become an astrophysicist, too. In school, Tyson's exuberance often landed him in trouble. One teacher even commented to his mother, "Your son laughs too loud." Aside from one straight-A report card in seventh grade, Tyson's academic marks never resembled those of your stereotypical Ph.D. in astrophysics. Tyson's early experiences show that the average American classroom experience is not necessarily a reliable indicator of success later in life. Outside-of-class activities that revolved around his passion for the universe, such as classes at the Hayden Planetarium and educational trips to observe and study the cosmos, proved much more beneficial to Tyson's motivation than school and parent-teacher conferences. An opportunity to deliver a lecture on the newly discovered Comet Kohoutek at the City College of New York at age fifteen gave Tyson an enticing preview of his career to come; merely eager to share his passion for the cosmos and knowledge of the comet with others, he earned a $50 paycheck and realized that it was possible to earn money by sharing the things he'd learned. Certainly it was far preferable to dog walking!

By his senior year at the Bronx High School of Science, Tyson was elected captain of the wrestling team and was editor in chief of the school's annual *Physical Science Journal*. The journal, the largest issue produced at the school in any subject at that time, contained a field report from an educational trip Tyson took to Scotland to map astronomical alignments of prehistoric megaliths with the Explorer's Club. Though he was thrilled to earn a grant to pay for the trip from the U.S. Department of Education, he is still resentful of the title conferred upon him upon receipt of the award: "gifted and talented." Tyson maintains that hard work and support from his loved ones are the real keys to his achievements, not an arbitrary measure of giftedness. "A more appropriate, though less catchy title might be the Department of Education's 'Office of Students Who Work Hard,'" he wrote in his memoir.

Work hard Tyson did, and he approached the decision of which colleges to apply to and attend systematically, counting the number of *Scientific American* contributors who had attended the undergraduate program of each school that admitted him as a student. Based on this data, he ultimately decided to go to Harvard University to earn a bachelor of arts degree in physics. "[Fifty percent] of my

NEIL deGRASSE TYSON AND CARL SAGAN

Neil deGrasse Tyson attended Harvard University to obtain his undergraduate degree, but he strongly considered Cornell University because of Professor Carl Sagan's presence on their faculty.

Carl Sagan was a hugely famous and influential astrophysicist. Involved with the United States space program since its inception, he experimented on many space expeditions and even briefed the Apollo astronauts before their flights to the moon. He received countless awards and recognitions for his contributions to science in his lifetime and was a pioneer of public science literacy with his accessible television program and accompanying book, *Cosmos: A Personal Voyage*.

Tyson's letter of application to Cornell University was bursting with such enthusiasm for the study of the universe that the admissions office brought it to Sagan's attention, and he wrote Tyson a personal letter inviting him to visit in Ithaca, New York. "Was this," Tyson recalled thinking in his memoir, "the same Carl Sagan who I had seen on NBC's *The Tonight Show*, with Johnny Carson? Was this the same Carl Sagan who had written all those books on the universe?" It was, and he proved to be kind, compassionate,

"We are made of star-stuff," wrote astrophysicist Carl Sagan, who popularized interest in the universe tremendously with his 1980 television series, *Cosmos: A Personal Voyage*.

and encouraging to young Tyson. Ultimately, Tyson ended up choosing Harvard over Cornell, but interacting with Sagan affected Tyson greatly.

"I never told him this before he died, but at every stage of my scientific career that followed, I have modeled my encounters with students on my first encounter with Carl," Tyson wrote. Appropriately, after thirty-three years, Tyson presented the follow-up to Sagan's beloved television series—*Cosmos: A Spacetime Odyssey*.

college education was in courses that had nothing to do with math or science. And I don't regret a moment of it. There's something to be said for when all parts of the brain fire at all times," Tyson said in an "Ask Me Anything" session on the Web site Reddit in December 2011.

Though Tyson's entering class at Harvard included children of luminaries and celebrities such as Caroline Kennedy, Tyson was far more interested in learning about the stars above. "My vote for the most under-appreciated discovery of the twentieth

The Bronx High School of Science, commonly known as Bronx Science, counts Nobel Prize winners, National Medal of Science honorees, and Pulitzer Prize winners among its graduates.

century," he wrote in the 1996 essay "Forged in the Stars," "is the realization that supernovae—the explosive death throes of high-mass stars—are the primary source for the origin and relative mix of heavy elements in the universe." This means that the raw materials that create everything in the known universe are ultimately provided by stars, just as the heat and light we require for life on Earth is provided by our sun. Truly, the universe that Tyson originally discovered in a planetarium show maintains its existence in an elegant and fascinating balance.

CHAPTER TWO

THE PATH OF MOST RESISTANCE

A s he continued his education in graduate school at the University of Texas at Austin, Tyson gained more mentors and learned about teaching as well as astrophysics. Tyson wrote in his memoir of Professor Gerard de Vaucouleurs, who showed Tyson, "No idea is too big to tackle. And no detail is too small to spend days or weeks investigating." Precision and patience, after all, are imperative to good science, and the biggest things in the cosmos are composed of incredibly tiny particles. The very universe itself was originally so small that it may be difficult to imagine. As Tyson wrote in *Origins: Fourteen Billion Years of Cosmic Evolution*, "Some 14 billion years ago, at the beginning of time, all the space and all the matter and all the energy of the known universe fit within a pinhead." In the present-day, much-larger universe, nuclear fusion in the cores of huge stars joins protons, neutrons, and

Tyson began his graduate education at the University of Texas at Austin, where he earned a Master of Arts degree in astronomy in 1983.

electrons—the components of atoms—to create the elemental building blocks that form all matter in the universe, including us. "Yes," Tyson wrote in the essay "Forged in the Stars," "we are stardust."

TYSON'S INSPIRATIONAL TEACHERS

Of course, human beings are far from the most important things that exist in the universe, except to ourselves. Humanity's collective sense of self-importance has often hindered scientific advancement. Though Greek astronomer Aristarchus of Samos first proposed the idea of a sun-centered solar system in the third century BCE, as Tyson explained in *Death by Black Hole*, the hypothesis was dismissed until Nicolaus Copernicus published a sun-centered model of the known universe about 1,800 years later in his work *De Revolutionibus*, at which

John Archibald Wheeler is credited with inspiring interest in general relativity in the United States following World War II. He collaborated on work with Niels Bohr and Albert Einstein, and coined the terms "black hole" and "wormhole."

time it was still so controversial that Copernicus himself noted that he expected to be "hooted off the stage with such an opinion." Humility is another essential quality to science, as new discoveries may easily eradicate years of hard work and long-held beliefs. Professor John Archibald Wheeler, a former student of Albert Einstein's, impressed this attitude on young Tyson in his class. "Wheeler was humble about what he knew and honest about what he did not know, leaving him quick to admit an error," Tyson wrote. "He always carried a supply of pennies in his pocket when he taught his graduate physics class. If you caught him making a mistake on the chalkboard, he would stop the class and publicly hand you one of these pennies. We all should live by these deep, yet simple, philosophies, but they are especially rare among leading scientists."

Professor Frank N. Bash directly influenced Tyson's own teaching methods. Impressed with Bash's method of teaching to the mind of the individual student, rather than the syllabus or chalkboard, Tyson wrote, "I am a better teacher, a better professor, and a better educator for my time spent as a TA (teaching assistant) under Professor Bash." Since a great deal of Tyson's life work over the years since has involved educating the public about the universe, many individuals indirectly owe a debt of gratitude to Professor Bash for his influence on Tyson's accessible teaching style. In an online crowd-sourced interview on the Web site Reddit in December 2011, Tyson offered the following advice to an aspiring science educator: "As for a career in science education, just remember that you sparking interest and enthusiasm in a student is far more valuable than the simple imparting of knowledge." In an interview on the same web site a month prior, he offered another enlightening quote about his teaching philosophy when asked what makes him happy: "Watching a person learn something new—not simply a new fact (those are cheap and easy)—but achieve a new understanding for how the world works. That's the only reward a (true) educator ever seeks."

SPREADING SCIENTIFIC LITERACY

In addition to his position as a teaching assistant in graduate school, Tyson gained experience as an educator through tutoring. While earning his undergraduate degree, he volunteered as a math tutor at a prison, aiding inmates who were trying to earn a high school Graduate Equivalency Diploma. These weekly sessions gave Tyson new insight into and compassion for the prisoners. Even under circumstances of life imprisonment or a death sentence, some inmates held the ambition to learn and improve their lives. Education can be valuable to anyone, he found, in any circumstance.

Though the scientific mentors he accrued along the course of his educational journey were incredibly influential to Tyson, it was the support and guidance of his parents that laid the foundation for his future career. "I must have had the first ever 'soccer mom,' except the activity wasn't after-school soccer, it was after-school astronomy," he wrote in his memoir. "With my telescope, camera, and other observing accessories, I would drag both of my parents (separately and together) in and out of cars, up and down stairs, in and out of fields, and to and from the library, all in the support of my astrohabit." Furthermore, weekend museum visits and purchases of affordable math and science books allowed Tyson to learn ever more about his interests. As an adult, Tyson has stated that his life's most important work is raising his own children. Being an astrophysicist and advocate of science literacy, of course, he feels it important to nurture his two children's scientific curiosity as well as their individual interests. "Whether or not they become scientists," he stated in an "Ask Me Anything" session for Reddit in December 2011, "they are no doubt scientifically literate."

RESISTANCE FROM SOCIETY

Tyson has been forthright in his writings and interviews about the negative effects of racism on his life and work. As a young man, neighbors often called the police when they saw him ascending to the roof of his apartment building with a telescope. "I shortly came to the shattering awareness that few parts of society were prepared to accept my dreams," he wrote in his memoir. "I wanted to do with my life what people of my skin color were not supposed to do." No one questioned Tyson's athletic achievements as he grew older, but when it came to his academic accomplishments, he was continually doubted and questioned. Throughout college, would-be helpful acquaintances and educators suggested alternative career paths to him, discouraging him from pursuing his dream of becoming an astrophysicist. He summed up years of bitter experiences in *The Sky Is Not the Limit*:

> *When combined with the dozens of times I have been stopped and questioned by the police for going to and from my office after hours, and the hundreds of times I am followed by security guards in department stores, and the countless times people cross the street upon seeing*

me approach them on the sidewalk, I can summarize my life's path by noting the following: in the perception of society, my athletic talents are genetic; I am a likely mugger-rapist; my academic failures are expected; and my academic successes are attributed to others.

The constant strain of fighting these attitudes placed an immense, intellectually draining emotional burden on Tyson. While working to complete his Ph.D., Tyson was interviewed by the local FOX news affiliate about solar explosions. When the interview aired that evening and he saw himself on the television, Tyson realized that he could not recall ever having previously seen another black person, aside from entertainers and athletes, be interviewed as an expert on a subject that had nothing to do with being black. When he earned his Ph.D. in 1991, he became the seventh black astrophysicist in the United States, out of four thousand nationwide.

"I do know that in spite of people assuming that I am intellectually incapable, I have retained enough confidence in myself to treat these encounters as the entertaining side shows that they are," Tyson wrote in his memoir. "I am certain, however, that many others do not share this same thickness of skin to withstand the constant onslaught of one's intelligence and ambitions. I occasionally wonder how I have survived it myself."

HUMAN SENSES VS. PHYSICAL REALITIES

In addition to teaching science, Tyson has written a great deal about the process of learning about the universe. Hearkening back to his rumination on Professor Wheeler's humble attitude, Tyson maintains that an essential component of learning about the universe is accepting the limitations of one's own senses. In the essay "Seeing Isn't Believing" in *Death by Black Hole*, Tyson wrote, "So much of the universe appears to be one way but is really another that I wonder, at times, whether there's an ongoing conspiracy designed to embarrass astrophysicists.

Telescope size and location are very important. Larger telescopes allow for bigger and better images, and high mountaintops help prevent atmospheric interference. Astrophysicists often travel to far-flung observatories, such as the Cerro Tololo Inter-American Observatory in Chile (*pictured here*), to seek the best views for their research.

Examples of such cosmic tomfoolery abound."
Widespread rejection of the sun-centered model of
the solar system, as discussed previously, is one such
example. To human senses, it appears that Earth is
motionless beneath our feet, while the planets, moon,
and sun move around us. Before it even occurred to
anyone that Earth might actually move around the
sun, it took a great deal of time for people to figure
out that Earth is actually round, not flat! These facts
seem obvious to us today, but try to imagine figuring it out with little better equipment than your own
eyeballs. With human senses, which are marvelously
adapted to help us live in our immediate environments but ill-suited to examining further-ranging
cosmic phenomena, it's something of a wonder that
our species has managed to discover so much about
the celestial bodies with which we share the universe.
To learn about many things in the cosmos, as Galileo
learned about the planets through his telescope,
we rely on ever-advancing technological equipment
to extend the range of our own senses accurately.
As Tyson put it in the 2001 essay "Coming to Our
Senses," "Discovering new ways of knowing has
always heralded new windows on the universe—
new detectors we can add to our growing list of
nonbiological senses. Whenever this happens, a
new level of majesty and complexity in the universe

reveals itself to us, as though we were technologically evolving into super-sentient beings."

Telescopes, of course, are indispensable to the work of astrophysicists. Tyson has observed the nighttime sky through many telescopes, but in his memoir he wrote that the Cerro Tololo Inter-American Observatory (CTIO) in Chile remains "closest to [his] scientific soul." Traveling to and observing at CTIO is something of a pilgrimage, requiring Tyson to first submit a proposal in hopes of being granted observing time. After making the schedule, an astrophysicist must hope for good weather, assemble detailed notes, make the long trek to the observatory's remote location in Chile, switch to a nocturnal sleep schedule in order to maximize time spent observing, and maintain a certain level of alertness while working in the thin mountaintop air. "On the mountain, each breath draws one-fourth less oxygen than at sea level, yet I am in computer command of millions of dollars worth of high-precision optics and hardware," Tyson wrote. "The stress forces me to reach a self-induced state of cosmic stimulation. Only while observing do I reflect on how many times in a normal day my mind drifts away from peak intensity through built-in mental pauses such as coffee breaks, lunch breaks, mail breaks, and the occasional stare out of my office window."

Tyson has spoken at many commencement ceremonies since delivering the address at his own Ph.D. graduation, encouraging graduates to face their own paths of most resistance with confidence and enthusiasm.

When Tyson was selected to give the graduation commencement speech to his Ph.D. class at
Columbia University, his inspiration stemmed from
observational time spent upon the mountaintop at
CTIO. "It is there that I obtained nearly all my thesis
data, and it is there that I reflected upon my life's
path through time and space," he wrote. Reflecting
on the decisions he made and actions he had taken
throughout his course to obtain his long-held goal of
a Ph.D. in astrophysics, Tyson realized that as a black
man who was constantly encouraged by other people
to choose another career, he had taken the "path of
most resistance." As he discussed in an interview on
the radio show and podcast *Bullseye with Jesse Thorn*
in 2013, however, this struggle to overcome obstacles
ultimately resulted in a richer, more satisfying career
and life. Tyson extends this philosophy to the learning process as well: the attempt to solve a problem
on one's own, though it may be frustrating and result
in many mistakes and wrong answers before arriving
at a solution, results in real learning and satisfaction
where shortcuts would not. "With the conferral of my
Columbia Ph.D., I had lived and fulfilled my dream,"
he stated, "yet I knew my life had just begun and
that my struggle would continue.

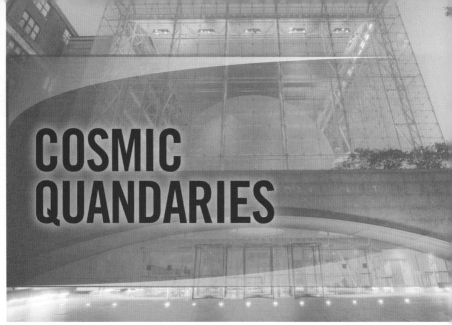

CHAPTER THREE

COSMIC QUANDARIES

In the years following his Ph.D. graduation from Columbia, Tyson worked in a split position at Princeton University and the Hayden Planetarium and wrote prolifically. From January 1995 to 2005 he wrote a monthly column for *StarDate* magazine, answering questions about the universe under the pseudonym "Merlin." Throughout the same time period, he wrote monthly essays for *Natural History* magazine, exploring cosmic topics as he saw fit. Material from these columns was eventually combined and revised into the books *Merlin's Tour of the Universe* and *Just Visiting This Planet* (from the former column) and *Death by Black Hole* and *Space Chronicles* (from the latter). These works collectively explore all sorts of fascinating cosmic subjects.

In the title essay of *Death by Black Hole: And Other Cosmic Quandaries*, Tyson described in gruesome (and fascinating) detail just what would happen to a person who fell into a black hole, and what does happen to wayward stars and gas clouds that wander into the vicinity of these devouring regions of space. As he noted, it would definitely be a spectacular way to go: "Where else in the universe can you lose your life by being ripped apart atom by atom?" In his memoir, Tyson noted that Professor John Archibald Wheeler, one of Tyson's instructors in graduate school, is widely credited with coining the term "black hole." Tyson offered this definition in 1994's "Confused Person's Guide to Astronomical Jargon":

This is what we call gravitational holes in space and time that look black. A black hole's surface gravity is so high that the speed one needs to escape from them is greater than the speed of light. Since light, itself, cannot escape then all hope would be lost for you if you happened to stumble upon one. Unlike a simple hole in the floor, you can fall into a black hole from any direction.

If a person did fall feet-first into a black hole, as Tyson explained in *Death by Black Hole*, the force of gravity at his feet would be greater than the force of gravity at his head, farther away from the black hole's center. The difference between these two forces of gravity at feet and head is called the tidal force, and

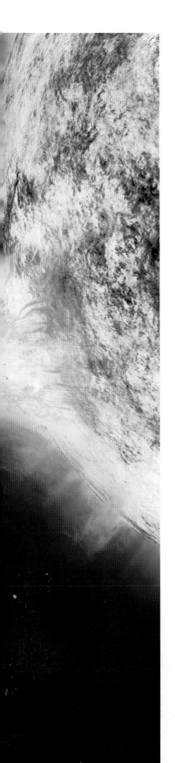

it's also how the moon affects the movement of the oceans on our own planet! Unfortunately for a person who fell into a black hole, the gravitational pull of a black hole is much stronger than that of our moon. The force of gravity at his or her feet would cause that person's acceleration toward the center of the black hole much more rapidly than the person's head, until he or she stretched so much as to rip in two! Then the two sections of the body remaining would be stretched and split, and the four sections resulting from that, and so on until even the protons, neutrons, and electrons that made up the unfortunate space traveler's atoms were pulled apart by the black hole's gravitational forces. Even worse, all of the particles would be traveling to the black hole's center, extruding our poor example through the fabric of space and time. "To all the words in the

An artist's rendition shows a black hole flaying the outer layer of gas from a nearby star. Bright quasar galaxies are formed when stars are slowly shredded as black holes "eat" them up.

SHARING SCIENCE WITH THE WORLD

Neil deGrasse Tyson doesn't just write about science in magazines and books; he also shares his knowledge of the cosmos on television, radio, and the Internet. Tyson has been active since early 2009 on the social media network Twitter, where he tweets miscellaneous facts about the universe, humorous opinions, and occasionally answers cosmic questions. Millions of people watch videos of his speeches and interviews on YouTube. He has appeared in television programs based on his books, in TV interviews on shows such as *The Colbert Report* and *The Daily Show with Jon Stewart*, and hosts the twenty-first-century reboot of Carl Sagan's landmark television series from 1980, *Cosmos*. On the radio show *StarTalk*, he discusses scientific topics with a comedic cohost and weekly guests drawn from pop culture. He has been mentioned himself as a pop culture figure in various TV shows and

Tyson is glad to discuss the wonders of the universe with anyone interested at academic conferences, on Twitter or Reddit, and even passing by on the street!

made a cameo on the comedy *The Big Bang Theory* and has participated in three "Ask Me Anything" interview sessions on the Web site Reddit. Tyson's involvement in many forms of popular media help forward his cause of science literacy, educating viewers, listeners, readers, and Twitter followers about the universe in a spirit of fun and curiosity.

English language that describe ways to die," Tyson observed, "we add the term 'spaghettification.'"

BLACK HOLES AS ENGINES OF SPACE

Though black holes devour everything that comes too close, their destructive appetites seem to serve a purpose: they are galactic engines, holding galaxies together. "The center [of a galaxy]," Tyson wrote in the essay "Galactic Engines," "is where you will find a galactic engine. The center is where you will find a supermassive black hole." The supermassive black hole at the center of our own Milky Way galaxy is dormant, meaning it isn't currently "eating" anything. Does a black hole stop eating because it becomes full? Astrophysicists think not. The best explanation to date is that a black hole only stops devouring once it has already vacuumed up all of the stars whose orbits came too close and it cannot "reach" anything else. Its gravitational force keeps other stars in orbit around its center but cannot suck them close enough to eat. We only know about these dormant black holes because the stars that orbit closest to them have much higher orbital speeds than those farther away. In active galaxies, however, a black hole may eat many stars per year. As Tyson explained, "The tidal forces of gravity for a black hole elongate the otherwise spherical stars," just as the body of the hypothetical person who was ultimately "spaghettified" would stretch upon falling into the black hole. Since stars are made of gas, the black hole shreds the star, pulling off layers of gas that fall into orbit toward the black hole. As these gases are slowed down in their fall by previous layers of gas, they give off heat, which makes them glow brightly. Active black holes gobbling up stars are the engines of quasars, extraordinarily luminous galaxies that are all billions of light years away from the Milky Way. The distance of quasars from our own observation point and currently available knowledge of black holes, Tyson suggested, indicate that "quasars and other active galaxies are just early chapters in the life of a galaxy's nucleus." This is the best explanation to date, though Tyson noted that it could change as new information is uncovered. That's science!

SUNLIGHT

Closer to home, something much more familiar lies at the center of our own solar system: the sun. As our parent star, it provides the light and heat that allows our species to survive. In "Journey from the Center of the Sun," Tyson explained how it does so. "The easy part," he wrote, "is the ray [of light's] 500-second speed-of-light jaunt from the Sun to Earth, through

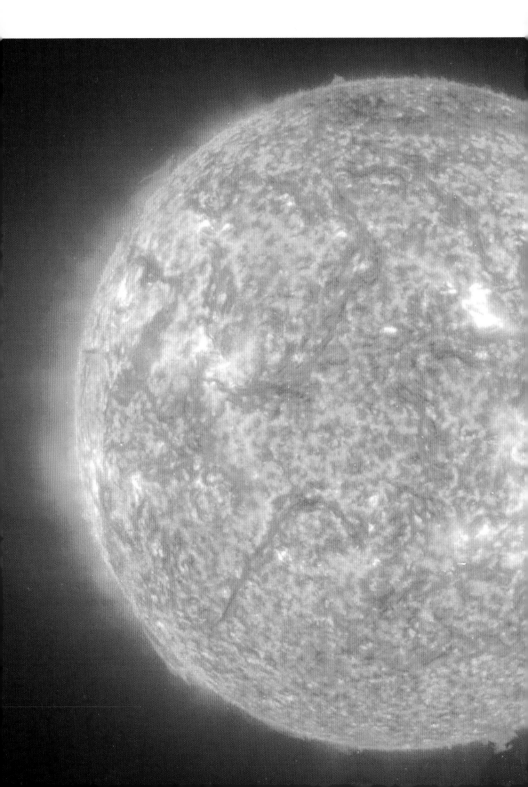

the void of interplanetary space. The hard part is the light's million-year adventure to get from the Sun's center to its surface." In the core of our sun, which is 15 million degrees Kelvin (about 27 million degrees Fahrenheit), hydrogen atoms speed around so quickly that they are able to collide with one another and form a single helium nucleus out of four hydrogen nuclei. This process of thermonuclear fusion creates energy in the form of particles of light, called photons.

Gas-filled loops over the region in which a record solar flare took place are visible in this 2003 photo from NASA.

These brand-new photons are born moving at the speed of light, 186,282 miles per second (300,000 km per second), and begin their journey out of the sun. Moving at the speed of light, you might think this would be a very quick trip, but that's not the case. Tyson explained the problem: "An undisturbed photon will always move in a straight line. But if something gets in its way, the photon will either be scattered or absorbed and re-emitted. Each fate can result in the photon being cast in a different direction with a different energy." In much less time than it takes you to blink, the average photon travels about one centimeter before bumping into an atom or free electron. Given a clear path, a photon could move from the center to the surface of the sun in 2.3 seconds. Given all the bumps it takes along the way, however, it takes approximately a million years for a single photon to escape from its birthplace in the center of the sun and travel out into space.

That's still not the end of the journey. On the way from the 15 million degree Kelvin center of the sun to the relatively cool 6,000 degree Kelvin surface (10,000°F), many of the original high-energy gamma-ray photons created in the center of the sun sacrifice themselves to birth multiple lower-energy photons. This creates X-ray photons, infrared photons, and the visible light photons that allow us to see during daytime. A single gamma-ray photon might create over a million visible light and infrared photons by the time its trek out to the sun's surface is complete. At that point, only one out of every half-billion photons travels toward Earth. As mentioned previously, this leg of the long trip is much easier, taking only about five hundred seconds (or eight minutes) to reach and collide with the surface of our planet. Tyson's comment on this incredible journey? "When I sunbathe, I do it with full respect for the journey made by all photons that hit my body, no matter where on my anatomy they strike."

Earth's distance from the sun, as Tyson discussed in the 1999 essay "Goldilocks and the Three Planets," is "just right" for water to remain liquid, providing the perfect environment for life as we know it. We would be foolish, however, according to Tyson, to imagine that planet Earth contains all of the life in the universe. There is an incredible variety of life-forms on Earth itself. A common garden snake would sound like an alien if described to someone who had never seen one before, and that doesn't even approach the level of difference between human beings and extremophiles, life-forms that thrive in exceptionally hot or cold environments, such as hotter-than-boiling mid-ocean ridges. These creatures never even see the light of the sun and would almost certainly survive a deadly asteroid strike that destroyed the surface life

The wide variety of terrestrial life on Earth is astounding, but all of it—from humans to whales, protozoa to snakes—are made from the same elements! Alien life-forms likely would be, too.

of Earth. In the essay "Life in the Universe," Tyson wrote that some estimates state that there have been more than ten billion species in the history of life on Earth. With this much variety on our own planet, it is highly probable that life exists elsewhere in the enormity of the universe.

EXTRATERRESTRIAL LIFE

Despite their portrayals in Hollywood feature films, Tyson continued in "Life in the Universe," alien life-forms would likely be very, very different from humans. However, this doesn't mean that aliens might not have anything in common with humans at all. "Aliens need not look like us to resemble us in more fundamental ways," Tyson wrote. "Consider that the four most common elements in the universe are hydrogen, helium, carbon, and oxygen. Helium is inert. So the three most abundant, chemically active ingredients in the cosmos are also the top three ingredients in life on Earth. For this reason, you can bet that if life is found on another planet, it will be made of a similar mix of elements." Planets that orbit stars other than our sun are called exosolar planets. The study of these planets, as Tyson discussed in the essay "Planet Parade" and the 2005 book *Origins*, is complicated by the fact that no human

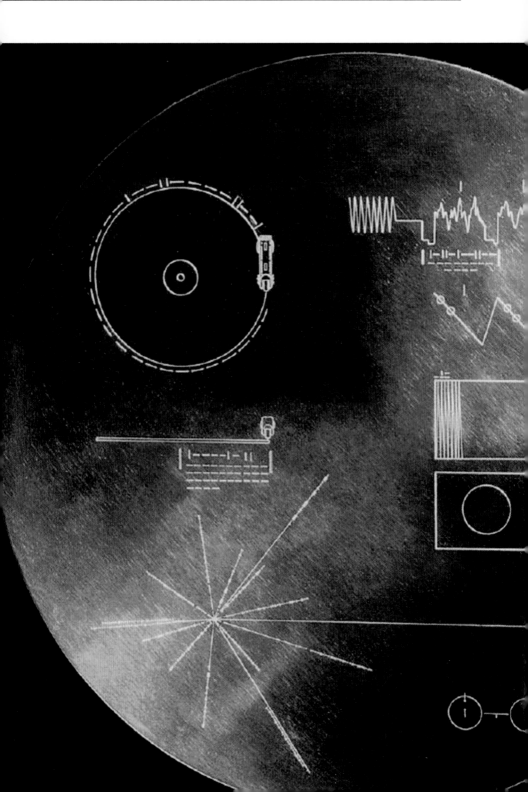

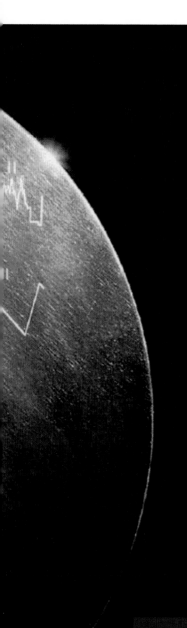

has ever actually been able to see or photograph one of these planets. Analyzation of the light spectra of a parent star led to the first discovery of an exosolar planet in 1995. In the years since, the number has risen past 150. The study of life elsewhere in the universe is called exobiology. As Tyson noted in "Life in the Universe," it is "one of the few disciplines that attempts to function with the complete absence of firsthand data."

Radio waves would likely be the best way to communicate with intelligent aliens, Tyson stated in "Life in the Universe," because of their ability to move across the galaxy without hindrance from interstellar gas or dust clouds. However, humans have only

Both *Voyager* missions carry a message stored on a phonograph record, a 12-inch (30 cm) gold-plated copper disk containing sounds and images representing life on Earth, in case the spacecraft encounter alien life-forms on their journeys.

developed this technology recently. If intelligent aliens had tried to contact Earth through radio waves a few hundred years ago, they would have received no reply. Humanity has previously made attempts to communicate with possible life in the universe using the language of science. In "On Earth as in the Heavens," Tyson explained:

> Such an attempt was made in the 1970s with the Pioneer 10 and 11 and Voyager 1 and 2 spacecraft, the only ones given a great enough speed to escape the solar system's gravitational pull. Pioneer donned a golden etched plaque that showed, in scientific pictograms, the layout of our solar system, our location in the Milky Way galaxy, and the structure of the hydrogen atom. Voyager went further and also included diverse sounds from mother Earth including the sound of the human heartbeat, whale songs, and musical selections ranging from the works of Beethoven to Chuck Berry. While this humanized the message, it's not clear whether alien ears would have a clue what they were listening to— assuming they have ears in the first place.

Far more likely is the possibility that we might discover simple, unintelligent life-forms—or evidence that they once existed—elsewhere than Earth. In "Life in the Universe," Tyson wrote that two good places to search are the dried riverbeds of Mars and subsurface oceans that are thought to exist under ice on Jupiter's moon Europa. If intelligent life exists elsewhere, it stands to reason that humanity will only discover it if both parties are looking for each other. As Tyson closed the essay, "The discovery of extraterrestrial intelligence, if and when it happens, will impart a change in human self-perception that may be impossible to anticipate. My only hope is that every other civilization isn't doing exactly what we are doing because then everybody would be listening, nobody would be receiving, and we would collectively conclude that there is no other intelligent life in the universe."

If you find any of these topics interesting, you should look into reading some of Tyson's essays. This section contains only a tiny sample of the hundreds of fascinating topics he has written about.

CHAPTER FOUR

PLANET EX

T hough Neil deGrasse Tyson's own professional research interests relate primarily to stars and galaxies, his name has become widely associated with controversy surrounding the status of a body within our own solar system. These events led Tyson to write a book about a subject much closer to home—that is, only about 5 billion miles (8 million km) from the sun: Pluto.

In May 1996, Tyson was formally appointed as director of New York's famous Hayden Planetarium (the very same facility that inspired his childhood wish to become an astrophysicist). His biggest responsibility in the new position was to serve as project scientist for the creation of the brand-new, $230 million Rose Center for Earth and Space, which would contain the renovated Hayden

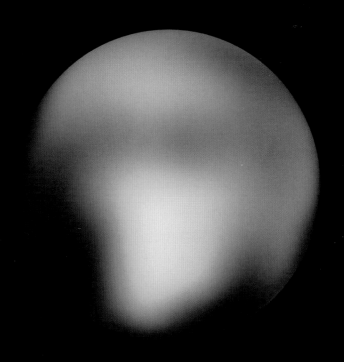

The dwarf planet Pluto may not have much mass or gravitational pull in comparison to the eight "legitimate" planets of our solar system, but disputing its planetary status earned Tyson a deluge of hate mail.

Planetarium as part of a new museum wing dedicated to the universe. To state matters simply, this was a huge responsibility. A great deal of time and effort on the parts of many experienced and talented individuals went into the design of the new facility. In this undertaking, the "shelf life" of various astrophysical subjects was considered. Scientific concepts that have long been accepted and are unexpected to be overturned in light of new developments— for example, that Earth orbits the sun—have a long shelf life and therefore may be communicated in permanent metal displays. Currently accepted ideas that are not as well-understood, or that might be expected to change with the advent of new data, have a shorter shelf life and would

The Hayden Planetarium in New York City took an enormous amount of time, effort, and money to construct. Its beauty reflects that of the celestial bodies about which it instructs visitors.

therefore be displayed in a less permanent format, such as exchangeable transparencies or video clips, to allow the museum to easily stay abreast of the most current scientific concepts. Deciding how to

organize each and every astrophysical concept and determine the longevity of all of these ideas about the universe was, as you can imagine, the tricky part, and Tyson wrote about the process in his book *The Pluto Files: The Rise and Fall of America's Favorite Planet.*

FROM THE LITTLEST PLANET TO THE KING OF THE KUIPER BELT

By the end of the 1990s, as Tyson detailed at length in *The Pluto Files*, some were already questioning Pluto's status as a planet, inspiring debate among planetary scientists. As more and more information about the different planets became available, their properties divided them neatly into two classes—the small, rocky, and dense terrestrial planets (Mercury, Venus, Earth, and Mars), and the large, ringed, gaseous, low-density, fast-rotating Jovian planets (Jupiter, Saturn, Uranus, and Neptune). Pluto alone was left classless, its properties vastly different from that of any other planet. In fact, with its small size, composition of mostly ice, eccentric orbit that crosses the orbit of Neptune for 20 years out of every 248 and that tips more than 17 degrees from the plane of the solar system, and the fact that it shares its orbital space with a great deal of icy debris, among others, Pluto seemed to possess more properties that resemble comets and asteroids than the other planets. Then, in 1992, another icy object (1992 QB1) was discovered orbiting the sun beyond Neptune. This object proved to be the first of many similar icy objects with tipped orbital planes existing in the outer solar system, just like Pluto. Within a few years of further discoveries, it became apparent that the solar system contains a "Kuiper belt" (named for astronomer Gerard Kuiper, who predicted its existence) of icy bodies in which Pluto resides. These discoveries alarmed Pluto-as-planet supporters such as Pluto's discoverer Clyde Tombaugh, who feared that if Pluto were "demoted" from planetary status, its prestige would be lowered and funds for its research and exploration would dry up.

Tyson, writing under the pseudonym of "Merlin" for *StarDate* magazine, supported Pluto's planetary status in 1997, writing, "Pluto is twice the size of Ceres, the largest known asteroid, and 50 times the size of the largest comets. When we consider that Pluto has a satellite of its very own it certainly gets Merlin's vote for full rank and privileges of 'planet.'" By February 1999, though, he had changed his mind.

PERCIVAL LOWELL AND THE SEARCH FOR PLANET X

"The most famous deluded experimenter in the history of astronomy," (as Tyson described him) was Percival Lowell, who makes appearances in many of Tyson's writings, including *The Pluto Files*, *The Sky Is Not the Limit*, and multiple essays included in *Death by Black Hole*. Wealthy Lowell loved to observe the universe, and his enthusiastic imagination showed him networks of canals on Mars and "spokes" on the surface of Venus. He claimed that both planets supported advanced civilizations. No one could ever confirm his findings, and in 2002 an optometrist proved that the Venutian "spokes" Lowell saw were actually shadows of the blood vessels in Lowell's eye, visible to Lowell because the optical setup he used to view the planet was similar to the opthalmoscope used by optometrists to examine the inner structures of the eye. The complex Martian irrigation system he thought he saw did not actually exist either.

Undaunted, Lowell founded the Lowell Observatory in Flagstaff, Arizona. He was deeply invested in the search for "Planet X," a suspected undiscovered planet that was thought to be lurking in the solar system beyond Neptune, affecting the orbits of Uranus and Neptune with its gravity,

Though Percival Lowell's ideas about Martian canals, surface features of Venus, and Planet X were all debunked, his legacy and contributions continue to benefit the field of astronomy.

and dedicated the remainder of his life to looking for it. Lowell was ultimately unsuccessful in this quest, which isn't surprising in hindsight, as it turned out that Planet X doesn't exist. Though Lowell passed away before his quest for Planet X was found to be futile, the search he began eventually led to Clyde Tombaugh's discovery of Pluto in 1930.

In an essay for *Natural History* magazine titled "Pluto's Honor," he stated:

> *As citizen Tyson, I feel compelled to defend Pluto's honor. It lives deeply in our twentieth-century culture and consciousness and somehow rounds out the diversity of our family of planets like the troubled sibling of a large family. And there was always something poetic about being number nine. As professor Tyson, however, I must vote— with a heavy heart—for demotion. Pluto was always an enigma to teach. But I'd bet Pluto is happy now. It went from being the runt of the planets to the undisputed King of the Kuiper belt. Pluto is now the "big man" on a celestial campus.*

THE PLUTO DEBATE CONTINUES... AND THEN ERUPTS

Concurrently, the International Astronomical Union (IAU), the professional society for the world's astrophysicists, was struggling with the same problem. It is the responsibility of the IAU to establish committees in order to formalize astronomical nomenclature and lexicon. Controversy began to brew, Tyson recounted, as "Plutophiles" in the planetary science community worried that the IAU planned to kick little Pluto out of the planetary club. In spite of his personal feelings on the matter, Tyson stated that he had no intention of imposing his own ideas about Pluto on the new Rose Center. On May 24, 1999, Tyson organized and hosted an expert panel debate at the main auditorium of the American Museum of Natural History in which he acted as a neutral moderator. According to Tyson's account, the panel was ultimately split on the issue, with one expert in favor of demotion (or "uncompromising iceballhood," as Tyson attested), two for split planet/Kuiper belt object status, and two in favor of planethood. Though no consensus was reached, the debate helped the Hayden Planetarium design team reach a decision. Ultimately, Pluto was not classified as a

planet by the Hayden Planetarium...or as a Kuiper
belt or Trans-Neptunian object. In the end, the planetarium exhibits merely grouped like objects with like
and declined to classify any of the celestial bodies on
exhibit as "planets" or "nonplanets" at all. This decision placed Pluto on display with a family of similar
objects in the Kuiper belt. This presentation, Tyson
felt, would provide maximum educational benefit
for visitors to the museum.

The new Rose Center for Earth and Space opened
to the public on February 19, 2000. Though some
media outlets commented on Pluto's absence from
the size comparison "Scales of the Universe" exhibit,
there was no controversy...for nearly a year, until the
New York Times ran a page one article on the Rose
Center on January 22, 2001. "Appearing in 55-point
type was the headline that would disrupt my life for
years to come," Tyson wrote.

"PLUTO'S NOT A PLANET? ONLY IN NEW YORK"

Though the full article provided scientific fact about
Pluto's place in the Kuiper belt and acknowledged
the ongoing controversy about its planetary status,
the inflammatory headline had done its work. Outrage
from offended parties ranging from planetary scientists to third graders flooded Tyson's e-mail, filled up

his voicemail box, arrived daily in the mail, and dominated media headlines around the world. Although the Rose Center's display decision was reached by expert scientific consensus, suddenly Tyson became known as Pluto's number one enemy. Tyson composed a media response in order to clarify the museum's position on the issue, and the team added a "Where's Pluto?" plaque to the Scales of the Universe exhibit in order to placate angry Plutophiles, but these measures did nothing, as Tyson put it, "to stave off the fulmination that would follow."

While Tyson wrangled with hate mail from elementary school students and sniping from colleagues, the universe and scientific research carried on unabated. More and larger Kuiper belt objects continued to be discovered, and the area beyond Neptune became ever more scientifically intriguing. And then, in 2005, something much more threatening to Pluto's planetary status than any museum display was announced: in 2003 three astrophysicists discovered what would eventually be named Eris, a body whose mass was 27 percent larger than that of Pluto. This called Pluto's status directly into question. If smaller Pluto was considered a planet, then Eris must be awarded planetary status as well. If Eris was not classified as a planet, however, it would, in Tyson's words, "drag Pluto down with it." The battle line was drawn, and the now years-old *New York Times* article had cast Tyson as an unrepentant Pluto-hater in the public eye.

SO, JUST WHAT CONSTITUTES A PLANET?

In light of all this controversy, an interesting (and, Tyson said, embarrassing) point arose: there was no agreed upon scientific definition as to what did or did not constitute a planet. The IAU formed an ad hoc Planet Definition Committee in attempt to come to some consensus before the membership convened to vote on whether or not Pluto should remain in the planetary fold. This committee recommended two criteria, that a planet (1) must orbit around a star, but not orbit around another planet, and (2) must be large enough for its gravity to shape it into a sphere, but not so large that it would trigger fusion in its core (which would make it a star). According to this definition, Pluto would have remained a planet *and* three more objects would have been added to the planet list: Ceres (an asteroid), Charon (Pluto's largest moon), and Eris. However, debate among conference attendees led to two additional criteria prior to the vote: (1) that the round body not be in orbit around another, larger world (disqualifying Charon), and (2) that the object must have cleared its orbit of wayward debris. As all orbital paths are cluttered with some debris this may seem confusing, but Tyson explained by comparing Pluto and Earth. Earth, Tyson wrote, far outweighs the sum of all the meteoroids it will ever collide with in its journey around the sun. Pluto, on the other hand, is outweighed by a factor of fifteen by all of the Kuiper belt comets cluttering up its path through space. This revised definition of planethood left the sun with eight planets, rather than twelve, and was corroborated by an IAU vote. On August 24, 2006, Pluto was demoted to the status of "dwarf planet," joining a new family of similar objects along with Ceres and Eris.

"In spite of widespread accusations to the contrary, I had no vested interest in the outcome of the IAU vote," Tyson stated in *The Pluto Files*, but he *was* interested in good science, which, despite the vote on Pluto's status, is not a democracy. The important thing, Tyson reminded readers in conclusion, is the search for consensus. "And until one is obtained," he wrote, "nobody should be defining anything."

CHAPTER FIVE

THE ULTIMATE FRONTIER

Neil deGrasse Tyson was born in the same week that NASA was founded in October 1958. As he explained in *Space Chronicles: Facing the Ultimate Frontier*, this meant that his earliest awareness of the world took place in the 1960s. This was the Apollo era, when the first manned missions to space took place and, in 1969, when United States astronauts became the first humans to land on the moon. Oddly enough, the moon landing was not very exciting to young Tyson. "The Moon landing was, of course, one of technology's greatest moments. At ten years of age, however, I found myself somewhat indifferent to the event," he recalled in his memoir. "It's not that I couldn't appreciate the moment's rightful place in human history," he continued, "I simply had every reason to believe that trips to the Moon would become a monthly occurrence. The ongoing space

Young Tyson imagined that traveling to the moon would soon become commonplace, but he was wrong. No human being has journeyed there since 1972, and only twelve have ever walked on its surface. In this image, astronaut Buzz Aldrin, part of the 1969 Apollo 11 crew, poses for a photo by astronaut Neil Armstrong, who was actually the first person to set foot on the moon.

program, with each mission more ambitious than the next, served as clear evidence of this future."

BUDGETARY ISSUES

Ten-year-old Tyson was wrong, though. The first mission to land on the moon was also the last to date, largely because funding for the space program has historically been primarily defense-driven. In chapter 11 of *Space Chronicles*, a transcription of a 2010 interview Tyson did for the podcast "Rationally Speaking: Exploring the Borderlands between Reason and Nonsense," Tyson stated that there are three justifications for spending large amounts of government money: "praise of royalty and deity," "the promise of economic return," and, of course, war. "When you're at war," Tyson noted later in the same interview, "money flows like rivers." The Cold War originally prompted the United States to fund space exploration in the 1960s. After the Soviet Union successfully launched a cosmonaut into Earth's orbit, which had never been done before, President John F. Kennedy made landing a man on the moon a national priority. Since the Soviet Union collapsed and peace broke out in 1989, Tyson explained, funding for the United States space program decreased drastically. Currently, other programs such as the China National

Space Administration and European Space Agency have pulled ahead of the United States in technological advancement and accomplishment.

Tyson, who served on two governmental commissions to investigate this issue—the Commission on the Future of the United States Aerospace Industry in 2001 and the President's Commission on Implementation of United States Space Exploration Policy in 2004—finds this trend to be disturbing for many reasons. When first asked to serve on a commission to study the health of the aerospace industry, Tyson was hesitant, but he grew concerned when research on the subject revealed that the industry had lost half a million jobs in the previous fourteen years. Then, shortly before the commission convened, the terrorist attacks of September 11, 2001, occurred. These events greatly impacted Tyson, who then and now lives a mere four blocks from Ground Zero, where the towers of the World Trade Center fell. "The events of September 11 magnified the importance of the commission's agenda: to recommend to the White House, Congress, and other relevant government agencies what strategies should be implemented to assist, or to rebuild, a failing industry—an industry that enabled a way of life and a level of security we have all taken for granted in America's post-World War II era," Tyson wrote in *The Sky Is Not the Limit*.

THE COSMIC PERSPECTIVE

The cosmic perspective comes from the frontiers of science, yet it is not solely the provenance of the scientist. It belongs to everyone.

The cosmic perspective is humble.

The cosmic perspective is spiritual—even redemptive—but not religious.

The cosmic perspective enables us to grasp, in the same thought, the large and the small.

The cosmic perspective opens our minds to extraordinary ideas but does not leave them so open that our brains spill out, making us susceptible to believing anything we're told.

The cosmic perspective opens our eyes to the universe, not as a benevolent cradle designed to nurture life but as a cold, lonely, hazardous place.

The cosmic perspective shows Earth to be a mote, but a precious mote and, for the moment, the only home we have.

The cosmic perspective finds beauty in the images of planets, moons, stars, and nebulae but also celebrates the laws of physics that shape them.

The cosmic perspective enables us to see beyond our circumstances, allowing us to transcend the primal search for food, shelter, and sex.

This famous image appears to show Earth "rising" over the moon's horizon. In actuality, the moon is tidally locked to Earth, so Earth does not rise and set over the moon as the sun does on Earth.

> *The cosmic perspective reminds us that in space, where there is no air, a flag will not wave—an indication that perhaps flag waving and space exploration do not mix.*
> *The cosmic perspective not only embraces our genetic kinship with all life on Earth but also values our chemical kinship with any yet-to-be discovered life in the universe, as well as our atomic kinship with the universe itself.*
>
> **-Neil deGrasse Tyson, *Space Chronicles: Facing the Ultimate Frontier***

After touring the world to investigate the state of other nations' aerospace industries, Tyson became angry—angry with his own country. "I got angry with America," he explained in *Space Chronicles*, "because advancing is not just something you do incrementally. You need innovation as well, so that you can achieve revolutionary, not merely evolutionary, advances." In a 2007 essay for *Parade* magazine entitled "Why America Needs to Explore Space," he noted, "In America, contrary to our self-image, we are no longer leaders but simply players. We've moved backward just by standing still."

WHY SPACE EXPLORATION MATTERS

Defense spending may be the most powerful motivator to convince the government to allocate funding to space exploration, but Tyson maintains that it is also important for the economic health of the nation. "Science and technology are the greatest engines of economic growth the world has ever seen. Without regenerating homegrown interest in these fields, the comfortable lifestyle to which Americans have become accustomed will draw to a rapid close," he wrote in "Why America Needs to Explore Space." In his 2012 testimony to the United States Senate on the "Past, Present, and Future of NASA," Tyson argued that space exploration inspired and energized the scientists, engineers, and technologists of America to great heights of scientific and technological innovation, which in turn encouraged economic growth. "During the Apollo era, you didn't need government programs to convince people that doing science and engineering was good for the country. It was self-evident. And even those not formally trained in technical fields embraced what those fields meant for the collective national future," he said. Excitement and discovery are key to innovation, and as Tyson has discussed in many writings, who wants to become an aerospace engineer when the job just offers the promise of designing a slightly more fuel efficient airplane than those of the previous generation? Without working at the frontier of technology,

progress stagnates, and aerospace is, as Tyson noted in *Space Chronicles*, a frontier of our technological prowess. Additionally, developments initially researched and employed in the service of space

Space exploration requires a number of talented people to fill many roles. In this image, flight controllers guide the International Space Station from their workspace on Earth.

exploration have spawned countless products and services that enrich human life in other ways. Lasik surgery, scratch-resistant lenses, cordless power tools, temper foam, cochlear implants, and miniature electronics are a few examples Tyson named in his testimony to the U.S. Senate. Furthermore, high-tech medical equipment and procedures such as MRIs, PET scans, ultrasound, and X-rays all operate on principles discovered by physicists and based on designs by engineers, he stated in *Space Chronicles.* "Epic space adventures plant seeds of economic growth, because doing what's never been done before is intellectually seductive (whether deemed practical or not), and innovation follows, just

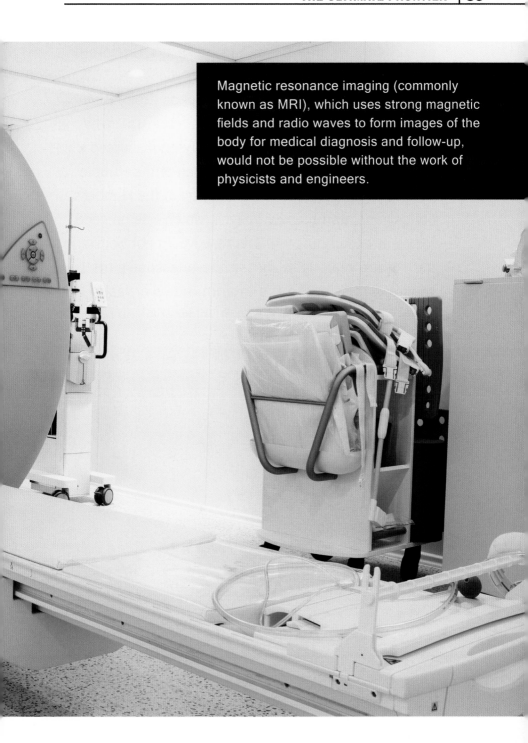

Magnetic resonance imaging (commonly known as MRI), which uses strong magnetic fields and radio waves to form images of the body for medical diagnosis and follow-up, would not be possible without the work of physicists and engineers.

as day follows night," he stated in his testimony to the Senate.

Even mistakes in the quest of space exploration can lead to benefits for the human race. In "Why America Needs to Explore Space," Tyson discussed a problem encountered upon the launch of the Hubble Space Telescope. A flaw in the design of the Hubble's optics generated blurred images, which was no good for its intended purpose. The flaw would not be fixed until three years later during the telescope's first servicing mission. In the interim, however, astrophysicists at Baltimore's Space Telescope Science

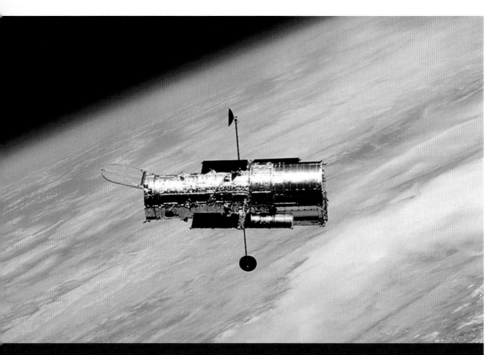

The Hubble Telescope has beamed hundreds of thousands of stunning cosmic images to Earth, to the benefit of researchers and the general public.

Institute were determined to make the best of the blurry images the telescope provided and worked hard to write image-processing software to help them identify individual stars in crowded, unfocused fields. Medical researchers at the Lombardi Cancer Research Center at the Georgetown University Medical Center

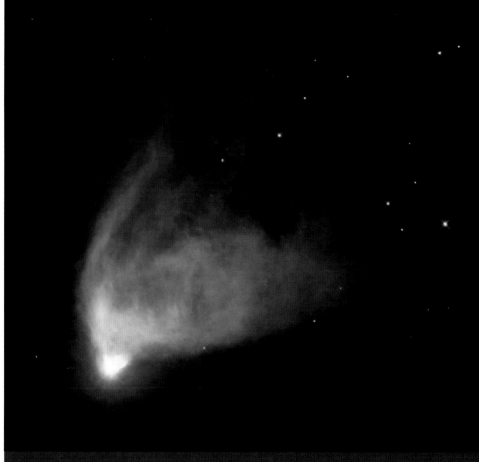

Images provided by the Hubble Space Telescope—even early blurry ones such as this one—allow observation of previously unobservable phenomena, giving us clues to mysteries such as the age of the universe and the existence of dark matter.

in Washington, D.C., Tyson explained, realized that the astrophysicists' struggle to identify stars in the blurry images was similar to doctors' efforts to search for tumors in mammograms. Funding from the National Science Foundation allowed the medical community to adopt the techniques developed by the astrophysicists working on the Hubble in order to assist in early detection of breast cancer. As Tyson put it, "Countless women are alive today because of ideas stimulated by a design flaw in the Hubble Space Telescope."

Though NASA's funding and activities have been greatly curtailed since the time of the Apollo era, some exciting missions are still underway. In *The Pluto Files*, Tyson briefly discussed the *New Horizons* unmanned probe. Launched in 2006, it is currently on its journey to fly by the dwarf planet and its moons. It has already sent back information on Jupiter, which it passed partway through its mission. In August 2012, Tyson carried on a Twitter "conversation" with the *Curiosity* rover en route to Mars (or, rather, the person manning its Twitter account). This back-and-forth was not only humorous, but informative. As Tyson tweeted, "Dear @MarsCuriosity, wait a minute. You travelled a 100-million miles in space & hit an area 12x4 miles? Cool. Way better than a hole-in-one." In 2010, Matt Lauer questioned Tyson about the *Cassini* spacecraft orbiting around Saturn on the *Today Show*:

"But Dr. Tyson, this is a $3.3 billion mission. Given all the problems we have in the world today, how can you justify that expenditure?" Rather than attempt to justify the project's potential scientific value, Tyson addressed Lauer's implication that the project was too expensive and responded, "First of all, it's $3.3 billion divided by twelve. It's a twelve-year mission. Now we have the real number: less than $300 million per year. Hmmm. $300 million. Americans spend more than that per year on lip balm." *Cassini* is still in orbit around Tyson's favorite planet, Saturn, observing its moons, its ring systems, and the planet itself. Unfortunately, some other initiatives, such as a return mission to the moon, have been cancelled.

PAYOFFS OF PAYING FOR THE JOURNEY INTO SPACE

Tyson maintains that space and space exploration are a deeply ingrained aspect of American culture. "If you ask me, 'What is culture?'" he wrote in *Space Chronicles*, "I would say it is all the things we do as a nation or group or inhabitants of a city or region, yet no longer pay attention to. It's the things we take for granted." As a kid, Tyson already took the moon landing for granted as a natural cultural progression. Today, as he points out, you can buy refrigerator magnets in the shape of the Hubble Space Telescope.

Many new car models are named for cosmic inspirations. Children decorate their bedroom ceilings with glow-in-the-dark stars. None of this seems notable to Americans because it's just the way things are—just part of the culture. "I'll bet you have a favorite picture of the cosmos taken by the orbiting robot known as the Hubble Space Telescope," Tyson wrote, even if you haven't thought about where the image came from. "I'll bet you can recall images from the rovers that have six-wheeled their way across the rocky Martian landscape. I'll further bet that you've seen some jaw-dropping images of the Jovian planets—the gas giants of the outer solar system—and their zoo of moons, images taken over the decades by the *Voyager*, *Galileo*, and *Cassini* space probes." These images have had such an impact on the American public that when a servicing

A well-known image of Jupiter, taken by the *Voyager* 1 spacecraft in 1979, allows us to see Jupiter's "Great Red Spot" and moon Io in previously unheard-of detail.

mission to fix the Hubble came under threat of cancellation in 2009, there was national outcry. The angry public reaction eventually saw funding for the mission restored. As we saw previously, the American people are also very attached to Pluto and did not respond happily when its planetary status fell under debate. Years after Pluto was officially downgraded to the status of dwarf planet, Tyson still receives hate mail from people who feel that his decision not to feature Pluto in the Hayden Planetarium's "Scales of the Universe" exhibit somehow contributed to this slight against their favorite faraway ball of ice.

If Tyson had his way, or were "the pope of Congress," as he jokingly put it in *Space Chronicles*, he would double NASA's budget. Perhaps this sounds extreme, but not as much as you might think. As he mentioned in his testimony to the Senate, two years of United States military spending exceeds the amount of government funding NASA has received in its entire history. Currently, he stated, NASA's annual budget is equivalent to half a penny on the tax dollar. By increasing that amount to a penny on the dollar, Tyson believes that the United States space program could achieve benefits beyond public imagining. Perhaps a better-funded space program could even save the world as we know it. As Tyson wrote in his memoir:

Suppose we interpret the word "defense" to mean something far more important than what standing armies and arsenals can bring. Suppose defense means not the defense of political borders but the defense of the human species itself. One needn't look far for a fast lesson in survival. When the Shoemaker-Levy 9 Comet slammed into Jupiter's upper atmosphere, it unleashed an equivalent energy of two hundred thousand megatons of TNT on the planet. At ten trillion times the destructive energy of the Hiroshima atomic bomb, this sort of collision, if it happened on Earth, would swiftly render the human species extinct.

REACHING FOR THE STARS

The dinosaurs were wiped out by an asteroid collision with Earth, and the same thing could happen to humanity. In spite of Hollywood blockbusters' varied solutions to this threat, in reality we would currently be ill-prepared to face it. Discussing the subject further, Tyson wrote that research of Earth's climate and ecosystem, viable space travel, and colonization of new worlds should be considered as a species survival insurance policy, but acknowledged in an interview in *Space Chronicles* that he believes that repairing Earth's ecosystem and figuring out how to deflect an oncoming asteroid is probably a more expedient solution to protecting life on Earth.

Even discounting the possibility of impending doom, Tyson firmly believes that space exploration and study are vital pursuits for the betterment of humanity. As he wrote in the 2002 essay "Where Even the Sky Is No Limit," "We need a mission plan where our curiosity guides our destinations. We need to share dreams worthy of a nation's commitment yet worthy of a child's capacity to imagine. And we know of no subject with greater power to achieve these goals than the prospect of reaching for the stars. Only in space is the sky not the limit."

1958 Neil deGrasse Tyson is born on October 5 in New York City.

1976 Tyson graduates from the Bronx High School of Science.

1980 Tyson graduates from Harvard University with a bachelor of arts degree in physics.

1983 Tyson earns a master of arts degree in astronomy from the University of Texas, in Austin, Texas.

1989 Tyson earns a master of philosophy degree in astrophysics from Columbia University in New York City.

1991 Tyson graduates from Columbia University with a doctorate in astrophysics.

1994 Tyson becomes a staff scientist at the Hayden Planetarium and research scientist and lecturer at Princeton University.

1995 Tyson becomes acting director at the Hayden Planetarium and begins writing monthly columns for *Natural History* and *StarDate* magazines.

1996 Tyson becomes Frederick P. Rose Director of the Hayden Planetarium.

1997 Tyson becomes founder and chair of the Department of Astrophysics at the American Museum of Natural History and begins overseeing the $210 million reconstruction of the Hayden Planetarium as project scientist.

2000 Tyson is named "Sexiest Astrophysicist Alive" by *People* magazine.

2001 Appointed by President George W. Bush, Tyson serves on the twelve-member Commission on the Future of the United States Aerospace Industry.

2004 *Origins: Fourteen Billion Years of Cosmic Evolution*, cowritten with Donald Goldsmith, is published. Tyson is appointed by President George W. Bush to serve on a nine-member Commission on the Implementation of United States Space Exploration Policy. His memoir, *The Sky Is Not the Limit: Adventures of an Urban Astrophysicist*, is published.

2005 Appointed by NASA administrator to serve on advisory council to help to guide NASA's scientific, technological, and budgetary steps forward in space.

2006 Tyson hosts *NOVA ScienceNOW* on Public Broadcast Television.

2007 *Death by Black Hole: And Other Cosmic Quandaries*, a revised collection of essays, is published.

2009 *The Pluto Files: The Rise and Fall of America's Favorite Planet* is published. Tyson joins Twitter and starts *StarTalk Radio*.

2011 Tyson does the first of his wildly popular "Ask Me Anything" sessions on the Web site Reddit.

2012 *Space Chronicles: Facing the Ultimate Frontier*, reflections on the United States space program, is published.

2014 Tyson hosts *Cosmos: A Space-Time Odyssey*, a follow-up to Carl Sagan's beloved 1980 series, *Cosmos: A Personal Journey*.

GLOSSARY

asteroid A rocky body orbiting the sun.

atom The basic unit of a chemical element.

black hole A region of space in which gravity is so great that not even light can escape.

comet An icy body that often displays a tail when passing near the sun.

cosmos The universe understood as an ordered system.

dwarf planet A new classification of bodies in the solar system, which includes Pluto, Eris, and Ceres.

electron A negatively charged subatomic particle-that, along with protons and neutrons, makes up an atom.

galaxy A system of millions or billions of stars, along with gas and dust, that is held together by gravitational attraction.

gravity A physical force that causes attraction between objects that have mass.

moon A celestial body that orbits around a planet.

NASA The National Aeronautics and Space Administration, responsible for the United States' civilian aeronautics and aerospace research.

neutron A subatomic particle of about the same mass as a proton but without an electric charge.

Neutrons are present in the nuclei of all atoms except hydrogen.

nuclear fusion A reaction in which two or more atomic nuclei collide at a very high speed and join to form a new type of atomic nucleus.

photon A particle of light created by nuclear fusion in a star's core.

planet A spherical body in orbit around a star that is large enough to clear its orbit of wayward debris.

proton A positively charged subatomic particle that, along with electrons and neutrons, makes up an atom.

quasar A particularly bright galaxy powered by a central black hole, thought to be an early stage in the life of a galaxy.

solar system A collection of planets orbiting around a star.

star A large celestial body made of gas that creates energy through nuclear fusion in its core.

universe All existing matter and space considered as a whole.

FOR MORE INFORMATION

Hayden Planetarium
81 Central Park West
New York, NY 10023
(212) 769-5100
Web site: http://www.haydenplanetarium.org
Operating out of the Department of Astrophysics at the
American Museum of Natural History, the Hayden
Planetarium's mission is to bring the frontier of
astrophysical research to the public through exhib-
its, books, public programs, and online resources.

H. R. MacMillan Space Centre
1100 Chestnut Street
Vancouver, BC V6J 3J9
Canada
(604) 738-7827
Web site: http://www.spacecentre.ca
This is a nonprofit community resource to educate,
inspire, and evoke a sense of wonder about the
universe, our planet, and space exploration.

Lowell Observatory
1400 W Mars Hill Road
Flagstaff, AZ 86001
(928) 774-3358
Web site: http://www.lowell.edu

Founded in 1894 by Percival Lowell, the Lowell
Observatory is an astronomical observatory open
to the public. It is a National Historic Landmark.

National Air and Space Museum
600 Independence Avenue SW
Washington, DC 20560
(202) 633-2214
Web site: http://airandspace.si.edu
Part of the Smithsonian, the National Air and Space
Museum maintains the world's largest and most
significant collection of aviation and space artifacts.

Science North
100 Ramsey Lake Road
Greater Sudbury, ON P3E 5S9
Canada
(705) 522-3701
Web site: http://www.sciencenorth.ca
This is an interactive science museum and education
center in Greater Sudbury, Ontario, Canada.

Space Camp
U.S. Space & Rocket Center
One Tranquility Base
Huntsville, AL 35805
(800) 63-SPACE (77223)

Web site: http://www.spacecamp.com
This educational program promotes the study of
math, science, and technology.

Space Center Houston
1601 NASA Pkwy
Houston, TX 77058
(281) 244-2100
Web site: http://spacecenter.org
Space Center Houston offers exhibits, attractions,
special presentations, and hands-on activities to
let visitors experience the story of NASA's manned
space flight program.

WEB SITES

Due to the changing nature of Internet links, Rosen
Publishing has developed an online list of Web sites
related to the subject of this book. This site is updated
regularly. Please use this link to access the list:

http://www.rosenlinks.com/GSW/Tyson

FOR FURTHER READING

Al-Khalili, Jim. *Black Holes, Wormholes and Time Machines*. Boca Raton, FL: CRC Press, 2012.

Billings, Lee. *Five Billion Years of Solitude: The Search for Life Among the Stars*. New York, NY: Penguin, 2013.

Briggs, Amy, and Peter Vesterbacka. *National Geographic Angry Birds Space: A Furious Flight into the Final Frontier*. Washington, DC: National Geographic, 2012.

Brown, Mike. *How I Killed Pluto and Why It Had It Coming*. New York, NY: Spiegel & Grau, 2010.

Carroll, Michael. *Drifting on Alien Winds: Exploring the Skies and Weather of Other Worlds*. New York, NY: Springer, 2011.

Chown, Marcus. *Solar System: A Visual Exploration of All the Planets, Moons and Other Heavenly Bodies That Orbit Our Sun*. New York, NY: Black Dog & Leventhal Publishers, 2011.

Daniels, Patricia, and Robert Burnham. *The New Solar System: Ice Worlds, Moons, and Planets Redefined*. Washington, DC: National Geographic, 2009.

Gribbin, John. *Alone in the Universe: Why Our Planet Is Unique*. Hoboken, NJ: John Wiley & Sons, 2011.

Jayawardhana, Ray. *Strange New Worlds: The Search for Alien Planets and Life Beyond Our Solar System.* Princeton, NJ: Princeton University Press, 2011.

King, Andrew. *Stars: A Very Short Introduction.* Oxford, England: Oxford University Press, 2012.

Lang, Kenneth. *The Life and Death of Stars.* New York, NY: Cambridge University Press, 2013.

Mortillaro, Nicole. *Saturn: Exploring the Mystery of the Ringed Planet.* Ontario, Canada: Firefly Books, 2010.

Penprase, Brian. *The Power of Stars: How Celestial Observations Have Shaped Civilization.* New York, NY: Springer, 2011.

Sagan, Carl. *Pale Blue Dot: A Vision of the Human Future in Space.* New York, NY: Random House, 1994.

Sasselov, Dimitar. *The Life of Super-Earths: How the Hunt for Alien Worlds and Artificial Cells Will Revolutionize Life on Our Planet.* New York, NY: Basic Books, 2012.

Scharf, Caleb. *Gravity's Engines: How Bubble-Blowing Black Holes Rule Galaxies, Stars, and Life in the Cosmos.* New York, NY: Scientific American/Farrar, Straus and Giroux, 2012.

Seedhouse, Eric. *Interplanetary Outpost: The Human and Technological Challenges of Exploring the Outer Planets.* New York, NY: Springer, 2012.

Sparrow, Giles. *The Planets: A Journey Through the Solar System*. London, England: Quercus, 2009.

Woolfson, Michael. *On the Origin of Planets: By Means of Natural Simple Processes*. Hackensack, NJ: Imperial College Press, 2011.

Zubrin, Robert, and Richard Wagner. *The Case for Mars: The Plan to Settle the Red Planet and Why We Must*. New York, NY: Free Press, 2011.

BIBLIOGRAPHY

Bullseye with Jesse Thorn. "Neil deGrasse Tyson on the Universe and the Path of Most Resistance." April 2013. Retrieved September 10, 2013 (https://soundcloud.com/bullseye-with-jesse-thorn /neil-degrasse-tyson).

The Carl Sagan Portal. 2009. Retrieved September 10, 2013 (http://www.carlsagan.com).

Tyson, Neil deGrasse. "Coming to Our Senses." *Natural History*, March 2001. Retrieved September 10, 2013 (http://www.haydenplanetarium.org/ tyson/read/2001/03/01/coming-to-our-senses).

Tyson, Neil deGrasse. "Confused Person's Guide to Astronomical Jargon." *Universe Down to Earth.* New York, NY: Columbia University Press, 1994. Retrieved September 10, 2013 (http://www .haydenplanetarium.org/tyson/read/1994/05/01 /confused-person%E2%80%99s-guide-to -astronomical-jargon).

Tyson, Neil deGrasse. Curriculum vitae. Retrieved September 10, 2013 (http://www.haydenplanet arium.org/tyson/curriculum-vitae).

Tyson, Neil deGrasse. *Death by Black Hole: And Other Cosmic Quandaries.* New York, NY: W. W. Norton & Company, 2007.

Tyson, Neil deGrasse. "Forged in the Stars." *Natural History*, August 1996. Retrieved September 10,

2013 (http://www.haydenplanetarium.org/tyson
/read/1996/08/01/forged-in-the-stars).

Tyson, Neil deGrasse. "Goldilocks and the Three
Planets." *Natural History*, May 1999. Retrieved
September 10, 2013 (http://www.haydenplanet
arium.org/tyson/read/1999/05/01/goldilocks-and
-the-three-planets).

Tyson, Neil deGrasse. "I Am Neil deGrasse Tyson—
AMA." Reddit, November 2011. Retrieved
September 10, 2013 (http://www.reddit.com/r
/IAmA/comments/mateq/i_am_neil_degrasse
_tyson_ama).

Tyson, Neil deGrasse. "I Am Neil deGrasse Tyson—
AMA." Reddit, December 2011. Retrieved
September 10, 2013 (http://www.reddit.com/r
/IAmA/comments/
ngd5e/i_am_neil_degrasse_tyson_ama).

Tyson, Neil deGrasse. "I Am Neil deGrasse Tyson—
AMA." Reddit, March 2012. Retrieved September
10, 2013 (http://www.reddit.com/r/IAmA/
comments/qccer/i_am_neil_degrasse_tyson_ask_
me_anything).

Tyson, Neil deGrasse. "On Earth as in the Heavens."
Natural History, November 2000. Retrieved
September 10, 2013 (http://www.haydenplanet
arium.org/tyson/read/2000/11/01/on-earth-as-in
-the-heavens).

Tyson, Neil deGrasse. "The Past, Present, and Future of NASA – U.S. Senate Testimony." March 2012. Retrieved September 10, 2013 (http://www .haydenplanetarium.org/tyson/read/2012/03/07 /past-present-and-future-of-nasa-us-senate -testimony).

Tyson, Neil deGrasse. *The Pluto Files: The Rise and Fall of America's Favorite Planet.* New York, NY: W. W. Norton & Company, 2009.

Tyson, Neil deGrasse. "Pluto's Honor." *Natural History*, February 1999. Retrieved September 10, 2013 (http://www.haydenplanetarium.org/tyson/ read/1999/02/01/plutos-honor).

Tyson, Neil deGrasse. *The Sky Is Not the Limit: Adventures of an Urban Astrophysicist.* Amherst, NY: Prometheus Books, 2004.

Tyson, Neil deGrasse. *Space Chronicles: Facing the Ultimate Frontier.* New York, NY: W. W. Norton & Company, 2012.

Tyson, Neil deGrasse. Twitter. Retrieved September 10, 2013 (https://twitter.com/neiltyson).

Tyson, Neil deGrasse. "Where Even the Sky Is No Limit." *Florida Today*, November 2002. Retrieved September 10, 2013 (http://www.haydenplanet arium.org/tyson/read/2002/11/25/where-even-the -sky-is-no-limit).

Tyson, Neil deGrasse. "Why America Needs to Explore Space." *Parade*, August 2007. Retrieved September 10, 2013 (http://www.hayden-planetarium.org/tyson/read/2007/08/05/why-america-needs-to-explore-space).

Tyson, Neil deGrasse, and Donald Goldsmith. *Origins: Fourteen Billion Years of Cosmic Evolution*. New York, NY: W. W. Norton & Company, 2004.

INDEX

ABOUT THE AUTHOR

Jennifer Culp is an author and former editorial coordinator for the *Southern Medical Journal* and managing editor for the *Journal of Clinical Densitometry*. Currently, she writes nonfiction for young adults and children.

PHOTO CREDITS